Mae Jemison

by Sonia W. Black

Photo research by Sylvia P. Bloch

For Brad, who always encourages me
to higher heights
— S.W.B.

Cover and title page photographs courtesy of NASA.

Text copyright © 2000 by Sonia W. Black

For information contact:
MONDO Publishing
980 Avenue of the Americas
New York, New York 10018
Visit our web site at http://www.mondopub.com
Printed in the United States of America
04 05 06 07 08   9 8 7 6 5 4 3

Design by Alfred Giuliani
Photo research by Sylvia P. Bloch

ISBN 1-57255-801-6

Library of Congress Cataloging-in-Publication Data

Black, Sonia.
    Mae Jemison / by Sonia W. Black.
        p. cm.
    ISBN 1-57255-801-6 (pbk.)
    1. Jemison, Mae, 1956- 2. African American women astronauts--Biography. [1.
Jemison, Mae, 1956- 2. Astronauts. 3. African Americans--Biography. 4. Women--
Biography.] I. Title.

TL789.85.J46 B53 2000
629.45'0092--dc21
[B]

00-042364

CONTENTS

Introduction

Date: September 20, 1992.

Place: Command Center, Kennedy Space Center, Cape Canaveral, Florida.

Time: 8:40:25 A.M. . . . 8:41:30 A.M. . . . 8:42:35 A.M. . . . and counting . . .

Event: Mission Control is monitoring the flight of space shuttle *Endeavour*. Launched September 12, 1992, at 10:23:00 A.M., *Endeavour* is headed home.

The sky over the space center is the bluest blue, clear and still. Suddenly a thunderous noise breaks the stillness. *Endeavour* pierces through the blue, through the soft clouds. Like a giant silver bird, it swoops downward toward Runway 33. It levels. It glides.

"Looks good in mission control," the shuttle crew is advised by the mission ground crew. "Twenty seconds to touchdown." 8:53:03 A.M. . . . 8:53:10 A.M. . . . 8:53:15 A.M. . . .

The landing gear is down and locked. The drag chute is deployed. Nose gear touches down. . . . 8:53:23 A.M. . . . *Endeavour* has landed!
Mission duration: seven days, 22 hours, 30 minutes, 23 seconds.

Mission Control radios the spacecraft, "*Endeavour*, congratulations on a highly successful and historic mission."

Endeavour rests on the landing

strip. A physician enters the spacecraft to examine the passengers. All are cleared. The door of the spacecraft opens.

Dressed in blue NASA G space suits and smiling broadly, the seven-member astronaut crew emerges one by one from the ship. Each one receives a hearty greeting—a hug, or a firm handshake, or a pat on the back—from proud ground crew members. The happy returning flight crew includes: Robert L. Gibson, Mission Commander; Curtis L. Brown, Jr., Pilot; Mark C. Lee, Payload Commander; N. Jan Davis, Mission Specialist; Jay Apt, Mission Specialist; Mamoru C. Mohri, Payload Specialist, National Space Development Agency of Japan; and Mae C. Jemison, Science Mission Specialist.

At five feet nine inches, 140 pounds, with short-cropped black hair and sparkling brown eyes, astronaut Mae C. Jemison stands out in the group. This has been an historic mission. It is the very first joint mission between the United States and Japan, and Mae Jemison has become the first African-American woman to fly in space. For Mae, this extraterrestrial journey is an incredible dream come true—a dream she had held onto since childhood.

Just who is Mae C. Jemison? How did she get to this place in history?

PHASE I

The Dream Begins

In February of 1956, Charlie and Dorothy Jemison learned they were expecting a baby. Charlie and Dorothy lived in the South in Decatur, Alabama. They already had two children, a boy, Charles, and a girl, Ada. Everyone in the family was excited about the new baby. *Would it be a boy or a girl?* they wondered. On October 17, 1956, they received their answer. "It's a girl!" they happily announced to family and friends on the day she was born. The baby girl was named Mae Carol Jemison.

The Jemisons always wanted the best for themselves and their three children. Like many families in the South at that time, they felt there were better educational opportunities in the North. So, when Mae was three years old, the Jemisons moved north to Chicago, Illinois. As their children grew, Charlie, a maintenance supervisor, and Dorothy, a schoolteacher, encouraged them to be all that they could be.

From the time she was a kindergartner, Mae knew what she wanted to do. Whenever anyone asked young Mae, "What do you want to be when you grow up?" she always had an answer ready. "I want to be a scientist!" she'd reply brightly. Frankly, some people thought little Mae had her head in the clouds. They thought her dream was really far out. Indeed, it was. You see, the kind of scientist Mae actually wanted to be was an astronaut scientist.

At night, Mae would look up at the sky all lit up with stars. She wondered about what was out there, way up in outer space. And she would wish: Star light, star bright . . . I wish I may, I wish I might . . . fly to the moon and stars one night . . .

Some people did not respond in a positive way to little Mae's future career goal, however. Once when the youngster proudly told her kindergarten teacher that she wanted to have a career as a scientist, the teacher said, "You mean a nurse, don't you?" At that time, people only thought of men as scientists, not women—especially not African-American women.

Comments like the one that her teacher made did not discourage Mae, though. She was not even discouraged by the fact that during her childhood there were no African-American astronauts—male or female. Actually, there were no female astronauts at all!

The National Aeronautics and Space Administration (NASA) was founded in 1958. In the early days of NASA, only military test pilots were allowed to become astronauts. And these were all males—all white. But even as a young girl, Mae did not see these things as obstacles. "That was just some silly male stuff that was going on," Mae remarked years later. "When I was younger, I knew that I was going to go into space. I just assumed that I was going to go." She saw no limits to what she could do.

PHASE II

School Days

Mae absolutely loved to learn. From the time she attended elementary school, she was an excellent student. She couldn't seem to soak up enough information about the world around her. Her nose was always buried in a book. She spent hours in the library reading or getting books on astronomy, anthropology, archaeology, zoology—you name it. She read science fiction and worked on lots of science projects. And she was fascinated with NASA's space explorations.

During the 1960s, there was a lot of attention on the space program. In 1961, President John F. Kennedy gave a memorable speech. In it he said, "I believe this nation should commit itself to achieving the goal, before this decade is out, of landing a man on the moon and returning him safely to the earth." Incredibly, with the *Apollo 11* space mission in July 1969, the world watched this amazing event happen. Astronauts Neil Armstrong, Michael Collins, and Edwin "Buzz" Aldrin successfully landed on the moon. The words of Neil Armstrong when he stepped onto the moon's surface and planted the American flag are recorded forever in history. Twelve-year-old Mae Jemison was glued in front of her television set when Armstrong stated, "The *Eagle* has landed. This is one small step for man, one giant leap for mankind."

Mae got goose bumps, she was so thrilled by the historic event. Afterward she read anything and everything that she could get her hands on about *Apollo 11*. "I had an encyclopedia about the different phases of Apollo," she recalled in an interview. Her interest in space travel deepened.

That fall of 1969, Mae Jemison entered Morgan Park High School in Chicago. After a class trip to a local university, Mae became excited about biomedical engineering. She thought about studying biomedical engineering in college. To prepare, she made sure her high school schedule included classes in math, biology, chemistry, and physics. She also reported, "I was the only girl taking drafting classes in my high school."

Mae received excellent grades in all her courses and was always on the honor roll. In between classes, science projects, working in a local hospital lab, visiting the library or the Museum of Science and Industry, Mae still found time for "generally being a teenager."

Mae loved to dance. Her mother had enrolled her in dance school from the time she was nine years old. Mae studied jazz dancing and African dancing, too. She showed off her dance talent by performing as a member of the high school's modern dance club. A gifted choreographer, Mae also made up many of the group's dance routines. As if the dance group wasn't enough, Mae was also on the school's cheerleading squad.

At home, if *Star Trek* was on television, you could count on Mae being in front of the television set. She loved to watch Nichelle Nichols as Lieutenant Uhura blast her way through outer space on the hit TV series. Nichelle Nichols is an actress who is African American. Though *Star Trek* was science fiction, watching Nichelle inspired Mae's dream all the more.

When she was just 16 years old, Mae Jemison graduated from Morgan Park High School with honors. She made her parents proud when she won a National Achievement Scholarship to Stanford University in Stanford, California.

As in high school, in college Mae was an eager student. She studied a lot of subjects. Now she took courses toward a degree in chemical engineering. She also took courses in African-American studies for a second degree. Mae was interested in learning all that she could about her culture, her people, and where she came from. She also wanted to learn about other cultures. So she studied other languages, learning to speak Swahili, Japanese, and Russian.

"Science is very important to me," Mae once explained, "but I also like to stress that you have to be well-rounded. . . . You have to find out about social science, art, and politics." With this belief, Mae was an all-around excellent student at Stanford. In addition to her academic studies, Mae had a lot of fun taking part in theater productions. Mae would choreograph and perform dance numbers for different college shows. She was involved with sports and student organizations, too. Mae was so well-liked and well-respected by the student body, they elected her as the first female president of the Black Student Union.

Multitalented Mae Jemison graduated from Stanford—with honors—in 1977. She received a degree in chemical engineering and a degree in African-American studies.

Around this time, Mae heard exciting news about the space program. NASA had changed its rules about who could be a part of their astronaut training program. Now women and minorities were allowed to apply, too—not just white male jet pilots. The organization had had to change its rules because of a new law Congress passed back in 1972.

The law said that companies could not refuse to hire people because of their sex, race, religion, or their birthplace. Now NASA was looking for people from all different backgrounds to train to work aboard their space shuttle flights.

This news made Mae very happy. You would think that now she would jump at the chance to apply to the training program. But Mae did not apply. She still very much wanted to travel in space one day. But there was something else she wanted to do first. Mae had decided to study to become a doctor. She longed to help heal sick people. And she thought, too, that her chances for becoming a part of the space program could only be improved if she were knowledgeable in many areas. So at twenty-one years old, Mae enrolled at

Cornell University Medical College in Ithaca, New York.

Though space exploration was not in her immediate plans, Mae's studies led her to explorations in other parts of the world. She was always eager to learn about different countries and peoples. Through the medical program at Cornell, she got that opportunity. Mae spent time in the Caribbean on the island of Cuba as part of a medical team. The team took care of needy people who could not afford proper medical attention.

Mae also visited Kenya, Africa, where she worked with the African Medical and Research Foundation, taking care of the sick. Then one summer, she volunteered to work at a refugee camp in Thailand in Asia. The people in the camp did not have enough food to eat. And the food they did have was not healthy for them. They suffered from malnutrition. Some of the people had tuberculosis. Some suffered with asthma. Others had dysentery. Mae helped to treat them for these illnesses and more. Living in foreign places and working with needy people was a valuable experience for Mae. "You learn a lot about yourself," she said.

In 1981, Mae graduated from Cornell. She received a Doctor of Medicine degree. Now there was a doctor in the family. Her parents never doubted for one minute that Mae could do whatever she set her mind to. "They always encouraged me," Mae remarked.

PHASE III
Doctor on Call

Now that she had her medical degree, Mae went to work at the Los Angeles County/University of Southern California Medical Center. At first she was an intern, a doctor who is supervised by another doctor with more experience on the job. In six months, Mae completed her internship at the Medical Center and was ready to tend to patients on her own. She then joined the staff of INA/Ross Loos Medical Group in Los Angeles, California, as a general practitioner.

In the following months, Dr. Jemison was busy seeing patients. She enjoyed her career as a physician, but she kept thinking back to medical school. She thought about the times that she spent abroad caring for the sick and the needy. She wanted to do more of this sort of work. So at the end of the year, Mae left her position at the Medical Group and joined the United States Peace Corps. The Peace Corps is an organization of volunteers who work with people in underdeveloped areas to help improve their living conditions.

In the new year, Mae found herself in West Africa. She was assigned as the Peace Corps Medical Officer for Sierra

Leone and Liberia. This was a big job. Mae was in charge of health care for Peace Corps volunteers and people who worked for the United States Embassy in these countries. Everyone on the medical staff reported to Dr. Jemison. As part of her job, Dr. Jemison wrote health manuals and guides for safe, healthy living. She instructed the volunteer staff on how to use the manuals when teaching the people. She was also supervisor of the pharmacy and the laboratory. She even participated in research projects with the Center for Disease Control (CDC) working to develop vaccines to cure different diseases. Mae was trusted with all these important responsibilities when she was only twenty-eight years old. She was younger than her staff. Some of them had a problem with reporting to someone so young. But Mae's self-assurance and know-how won their respect.

Altogether, Mae spent over two years in the Peace Corps. It had been a really rewarding experience for her. "I've gotten much more out of what I have done than the people I was supposed to be helping," she remarked to one reporter. "I learned a lot from that experience," she said.

Satisfied that she'd done a good job, Mae returned to Los Angeles where she worked as a physician with CIGNA Health Plans. But her adventurous spirit was still very much alive. Mae looked for new challenges. There was one burning desire that had not been fulfilled as yet. She still longed to travel in space. At this point, Mae felt she had gained enough education and work experience to qualify for NASA's space training program. She was ready to apply.

Dr. Mae C. Jemison was at work in her Los Angeles doctor's office when NASA called with the incredible news that she had been accepted into the astronaut program.

During the year-long training program in preparation for their exciting space flight in the space shuttle *Endeavour*, astronauts Mae Jemison and N. Jan Davis mastered how to maneuver in zero-gravity aboard NASA's KC-135 zero-gravity aircraft.

One of the many things Mae was introduced to during training was how to operate sophisticated camera equipment used for space photography.

As part of the very intense astronaut-training program, Mae also learned how to skillfully handle a parachute.

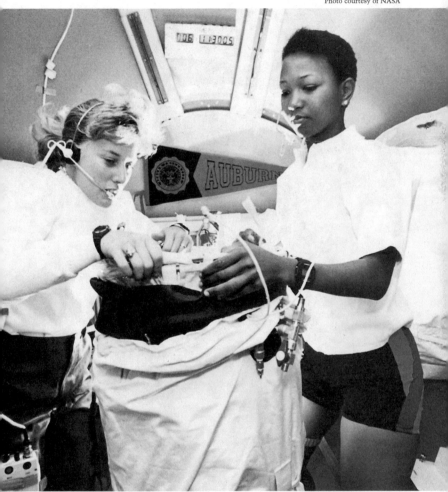

Mission specialists N. Jan Davis and Mae Jemison worked cooperatively in Spacelab J. "Teamwork," says Mae, "is very important in accomplishing a task."

Before the actual flight, the astronauts spent time aboard *Endeavou* in an effort to familiarize themselves with the spacecraft. Here, Dr. Mae Jemison intently examines the interior of Spacelab J.

The seven-member astronaut crew of the historic mission.
Pictured are (left to right, front) Jay Apt and Curtis L. Brown;
and (left to right, rear) N. Jan Davis, Mark C. Lee, Robert L.
Gibson, Mae C. Jemison, and Mamoru C. Mohri.

Astronauts at work. Each crew member had specific duties to perform in the Spacelab. They floated in zero-gravity while doing their work. Among other things, Mae was in charge of an experiment with frogs.

Say, Cheese! Mae Jemison and the rest of the astronaut crew take a break from working to pose for a group shot inside the spacelab

Once accustomed to the atmosphere of zero-gravity, mission specialist Mae Jemison got a kick out of "floating" about aboard the space shuttle *Endeavour*.

As the first African-American female astronaut to travel in space, Mae Jemison's childhood dream—and the dream of many other people—finally came true.

PHASE IV

A Dream Comes True

In October 1985, Mae sent off her application for admittance to the astronaut training program. While she waited to hear back from NASA, believe it or not, Mae enrolled at the University of California for night courses in engineering. Knowing more about engineering would further improve her chances of getting into the program. But, Mae was not admitted to the space program. This would turn out to be the worst time in NASA's history. Soon after Mae submitted her application, NASA experienced a terrible tragedy.

It was the morning of January 28, 1986—a freezing cold winter morning in Florida. At the Kennedy Space Center, NASA personnel were readying the launch of Orbiter *Challenger*. Mission 51-L would be the *Challenger*'s 10th flight into space. It would be NASA's 25th space shuttle mission. And it would be the first time that a civilian, someone who was not a trained astronaut, would be aboard a space flight. That someone was a schoolteacher named Christa McAuliffe from Concord, New Hampshire. There was a lot of attention on this flight because of

Christa. Everyone on Earth followed all the news about this *Challenger* flight.

Five times before, Mission 51-L had been scheduled for launch. And five times the launch had been delayed, all due to bad weather. NASA had never before launched a spacecraft in weather as cold as it was on this day. The temperature on Launch Pad 39B where *Challenger* sat was 36° F. Nevertheless, at 11:38 A.M. Eastern Standard Time, *Challenger* blasted up and away, leaving a long trail of thick, swirling smoke.

Barely 73 seconds later, disaster struck. Before disbelieving eyes, *Challenger* exploded in flight! All seven crew members aboard were killed instantly. The space program would be suspended indefinitely.

Like the rest of the world, Mae Jemison felt very sad about the terrible accident. But it didn't cause her to give up her dream. She knew all the risks involved, but she still wanted to fly in space. She was not afraid. "I never lost interest in the program," she reported.

Mae continued her work at CIGNA and waited patiently for NASA to resume the program. When they began again, in October 1986, she wasted no time in reapplying. For NASA personnel, the selection process would not be an easy one. About 2,000 qualified people applied to the astronaut program. Mae hoped she would be one of the chosen applicants.

Several months later, in February 1987, Mae was busy at work in her Los

Angeles office when she received a long distance phone call from Houston, Texas. *It must be the space center*, Mae thought. And it was. The call came from the Johnson Space Center. This is where astronauts are trained for space flights.

"Congratulations, Dr. Jemison!" the official on the telephone said to Mae. He had the best news to deliver. NASA was impressed with Mae's application. Dr. Jemison was being invited to the Johnson Space Center. Here she would be interviewed and put through all sorts of medical examinations and physical tests to see if she indeed qualified as an astronaut candidate. Mae's bright smile told everyone that she was thrilled.

PHASE V

Astronaut-in-Training

When Mae visited the Johnson Space Center, she passed all the tests with flying colors. So did many other applicants. The final selection was still to be decided. Mae waited for news.

On June 4, 1987, while at work on a break from tending to patients, Mae received the all-important call from NASA. The caller happily reported that she had indeed been accepted into the astronaut program. Mae Jemison would be the first African-American female to have received such an honor. She had been one of only 15 candidates chosen from the approximately 2,000 applicants. Mae had every reason to be proud. Her hard work and dedication had paid off.

"I was very excited," Mae remembered. She also humbly pointed out to admirers, "I'm not the first African-American woman who had the skills, the talent, the desire to be an astronaut. I happen to be the first one that NASA selected."

The year-long training program took place in Houston. It was intense work, but Mae came through like a champ.

She learned all about the space shuttle. The United States had introduced this brand-new type of spacecraft in 1981. The shuttle, unlike previous spacecrafts, could be used over and over again. It was a lot like an airplane only it was a thousand times more powerful. Mae learned everything about the different types of equipment on board the shuttle and how they operated. But that was not all. Training involved a whole lot more.

Mae and the other astronaut candidates spent many hours in NASA's "zero-gravity" training aircraft. The group had to learn how to function in an atmosphere like there is in outer space. In space there is less gravity than there is here on Earth. Gravity is what keeps us on the ground. The lack of gravity in space causes people and things to float all about and not have the control that we have on Earth. Inside, the zero-gravity aircraft is designed to imitate the atmosphere in space. The candidates had to get used to the lack of gravity and to floating in all sorts of positions. They learned to complete different tasks as they floated. After many hours of training, Mae and her fellow students got the hang of it.

The candidates did exercises in water-survival training, in how to survive in the wilderness, and how to adapt to living in small spaces. Among other things, they also learned how to use a parachute. To Mae, the most valuable lesson of all was learning the importance of teamwork in space travel. "Teamwork becomes important whenever you want to get a job done because there are very few things that any one of us can do by ourselves," Mae explained in an instructional video.

After a year of grueling training, in August 1988, Dr. Mae Jemison completed the program. She received a new title, mission specialist astronaut. Astronaut Jemison did not get assigned to fly on a space mission right away. There was a long list of astronauts before her who were waiting to get their chance to travel to space. Mae had to wait her turn. In the meantime, she had other jobs at NASA. Her first job was working as a representative at the astronaut office at Kennedy Space Center. Some of her duties included work preparing space shuttles that were about to be launched. She would check payloads, the cargo that would be on the shuttle. She also checked computer software in the shuttle lab. And she even worked launch countdown.

Finally, in 1989, Mae received the long-awaited assignment. She would be a science specialist aboard a mission on space shuttle *Endeavour*. *Endeavour* was the latest addition to NASA's fleet of shuttle vehicles. The spacecraft got its name through a national competition held in elementary and secondary schools. The winning students named the orbiter after a long-ago ship whose commander was James Cook, an 18th-century British explorer. He was a navigator and astronomer as well.

The newly built, newly named *Endeavour* arrived at Kennedy Space Center in May of 1991. Weighing 78 tons (70 metric tons) and measuring 122 feet (37 meters) long and 78 feet (23 meters) wide, the ship was built with more advanced equipment than NASA's other three orbiters at the time. With its new technology, *Endeavour* was capable of staying in space for as long as 28 days. On its very first flight out in May 1992, on Mission STS-49, *Endeavour* was a huge success. It rescued a communications satellite that had been stranded in space. This would be *Endeavour*'s second launch. It would be an equally memorable mission.

The mission was named STS-47 Spacelab J. Spacelab J was the name given to a laboratory that would be on board the shuttle. The main purpose of this shuttle mission was to conduct scientific experiments in life sciences in

Spacelab J. The "J" was for Japan. The United States and Japan had worked together to develop the different experiments. Japan helped to pay for the cost of the mission and sent along astronaut Mamoru G. Mohri as a member of the shuttle crew. This was a first. These two great nations had never worked together like this before.

The launch of the historic mission had been scheduled for the summer of 1992. "We worked on the mission for over three years as a flight crew," Mae remembered. After some schedule changes, launch day finally arrived—September 12, 1992.

Astronaut Jemison was more than ready for this way-out adventure. She dressed in her bright orange space suit and strode proudly with her teammates toward *Endeavour*. With each step, Mae realized her lifelong dream was about to come true.

PHASE VI

Into the Wild Blue Yonder

Strapped into her seat inside the shuttle, Mae waited breathlessly for the launching. She was filled with excitement, aware of each minute ticking away. Then the countdown began. 10 . . . 9 . . . 8 . . . Mae was a little bit nervous. Her heart raced. She could feel each anxious breath. 7 . . . 6 . . . 5 . . . 4 . . . But she was smiling from ear to ear.

3 . . . 2 . . . 1 . . . "And we have LIFT OFF!" The exact time, 10:23 A.M.

Endeavour blasted off the launch pad and roared upward, deep and deeper still into the sky. Pinned back into her seat from the sheer force of gravity against the speeding aircraft, Mae could hardly believe it was actually happening. Here she was, the first African-American woman astronaut heading into space. "It was the realization of many, many dreams of many people," Mae told one journalist.

Proud as could be, Mae had taken on board several items that were very meaningful to her. Because of her love and appreciation of dancing, she took a poster from the Alvin Ailey Dance Company. An honorary member of Alpha Kappa Alpha Sorority, she also took on board an Alpha Kappa Alpha Sorority banner. She even brought along the flag of the Organization of African Unity, symbolic of her cultural background.

As the shuttle hurled into outer space, incredibly, one of the first sights Mae saw below was her hometown, the city of Chicago. As they sped further away, Mae was amazed at the view of the earth below. "The earth was gorgeous," she reported. "There was a blue iridescent glow about the planet that was tremendous."

The astronauts couldn't spend a whole lot of time sightseeing, though. They all had jobs to do. Those on the payload crew had to get started on the mission of this spaceflight—conducting many different scientific experiments.

Mae Jemison was part of the payload crew. The cargo this time included frogs and frogs' eggs, fruit flies, Japanese koi fish (carp), and hornets for experiments.

Many of the experiments were set up to understand how the human body adapted to weightlessness in space. Others were to see how animals reacted to living in space. The astronauts got a lot of help from the ground crew.

The ground crew is made up of hundreds of scientists and specialists at mission control. From the control room these scientists direct the astronauts every day—hour by hour, minute by minute—as to what to do. "As science mission specialist, I was responsible for being the eyes, ears, and hands in space of a scientist on the ground," Mae explained to a video audience. "The ground crew are the ones who train us and make sure everything is going correctly."

The payload crew worked round-the-clock conducting experiments. They worked in two shifts. Mae worked the night shift. One experiment she headed up was studying cell biology in frogs. Frogs' eggs were hatched in zero gravity. Mae followed the development of tadpoles that came from these eggs. She had to compare the growth and behavior of these tadpoles to ones born on Earth. The results were that the tadpoles hatched in space developed normally. When they were returned to Earth, Mae reported, "They had turned into frogs."

The astronauts also studied the behavior of hornets. Would the bees build nests in space, for example? Most of the bees died. The ones that survived did not build nests.

What about humans? How does the human body react to living in space? It's been discovered that one of the effects of humans living in space is the loss of calcium in the bones. Previous studies had determined that women astronauts lose more calcium than the men do. On this flight, Mae took part in studies to help find an eventual solution to this problem.

Many astronauts also suffer from motion sickness in space. Because of the weightless atmosphere, body fluids travel toward the upper body. This may cause headaches, puffiness in the face, constant vomiting, and dizziness, among other discomforts. Mae took part in an experiment called biofeedback, a technique for controlling these symptoms without medication.

While the other astronauts took medicine for their motion sickness, Mae did not. Whenever she felt symptoms coming on, she would try and control her body's response naturally. She might meditate, concentrating really hard on making the symptoms go away. Or, she might do deep breathing exercises. She was hooked up to all sorts of electronic equipment that monitored her blood pressure, temperature, heart rate, and breathing. Mae kept careful notes of all the symptoms and the calming methods she used to overcome them. This would help NASA's doctors and scientists figure out if medicine or biofeedback was best to help astronauts fight off motion sickness in space.

Altogether the *Endeavour* crew conducted over 47 experiments. It was non-stop work. Mae described the typical daily routine to a young reporter. "We'd wake up, brush our teeth, wash up and get dressed," she said. "Then we'd go back to the space lab and do our work, eat lunch, go back and do more experiments." But there were moments of relaxation, too. During these restful periods, Mae would read or listen to music, or just gaze out the window at the stars. She couldn't help but remember a time long ago when she looked out another window—and dreamed dreams of reaching the stars one day.

After the many experiments, spending almost eight days in space, traveling 3.3 million miles (5 million kilometers), and completing 127 orbits around the earth, *Endeavour* headed home.

PHASE VII

Back Down to Earth

It was quite some time after Dr. Mae Jemison's return to Earth that her feet actually touched down. Her spirits soared as her hometown of Chicago honored her for her memorable achievement. There were six days of grand parades and other celebrations. Mae made special appearances and gave speeches about her incredible space journey.

Many awards followed that year and in later years as well, including the American Black Achievement Awards' Trailblazer Award and the Ebony Black Achievement Award. In Detroit, Michigan, the Mae C. Jemison Academy, an alternative public school, was dedicated to her. Then in 1993, she was inducted into the National Women's Hall of Fame in Seneca Falls, New York.

Always seeking new challenges, six months after her historic flight, Dr. Mae Jemison resigned from NASA. She joined the faculty at Dartmouth College in New Hampshire to teach space technology. In the meantime, Dr. Jemison still had a strong desire to help improve conditions in developing countries. To fulfill this mission, she started her own company, The Jemison Group, Inc.

Based in Houston, Texas, the science and technology company works on projects such as satellite communication systems and electricity-generating solar equipment. With satellite communication, health care can be delivered very quickly to poor areas. In places where there is no oil or coal, solar energy can be used to do the same job as these fuels.

Mae's company is involved in other positive things, too. She believes that science education is very, very important for today's youth. So together with other companies, in 1994, The Jemison Group sponsored the first of an annual International Science Camp called The Earth We Share. Students from the United States and abroad were selected to participate in the four-week program. The students learned about different science topics through interesting hands-on experiments.

The busy Dr. Jemison does find time to enjoy hobbies such as photography, reading science fiction novels, collecting African art—and she dances. Still she never misses a step in her goal to develop young people's interest in science and technology. Mae accepts as many invitations as she can to visit different schools and speak to students. She tells them of a future—a new millennium—brimming with opportunities for them to explore. She encourages them all—boys and girls of every race—to reach for the stars and not limit their ambitions. She points to her participation in the space program as an example that "all peoples of the world have astronomers, physicists, and explorers." Most importantly,

Mae Jemison—doctor, scientist, astronaut—advises, "Don't let anyone rob you of your imagination, your creativity, or your curiosity."